D1609180

Strange and Wonderful Aircraft

Harvey Weiss

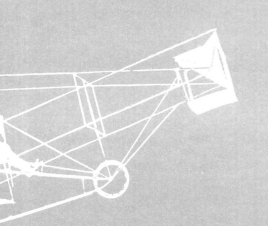

Houghton Mifflin Company • Boston 1995

Central Islip Public Library
33 Hawthorne Avenue
Central Islip, NY 11722-2498

141 5583

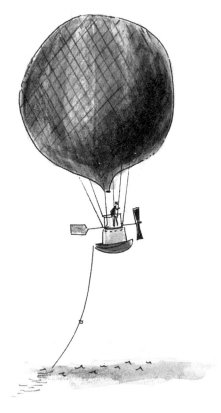

The balloon shown above was planned for a transatlantic flight. But the brave aeronaut, Charles Green, who intended to make this trip in 1840, evidently thought better of it, and the voyage never occurred. (An *aeronaut* is a person who operates or travels in an airship or balloon.)

The author is indebted to the National Air and Space Museum/ Smithsonian Institution for their assistance and for permission to reproduce photographs in their collection.

Copyright © 1995 by Harvey Weiss

All rights reserved. For information about permission to reproduce selections from this book, write to Permissions, Houghton Mifflin Company, 215 Park Avenue South, New York, New York 10003.

Library of Congress Cataloging-in-Publication Data

Weiss, Harvey.
  Strange and wonderful aircraft / by Harvey Weiss.
    p. cm.
  ISBN 0-395-68716-0
  1. Flight — History — Juvenile literature.   [1. Flight — History.]
I. Title.
TL547.W38   1995   94-3788
629.13 — dc20   CIP
              AC

Printed in the United States of America
HOR 10 9 8 7 6 5 4 3 2 1

CONTENTS

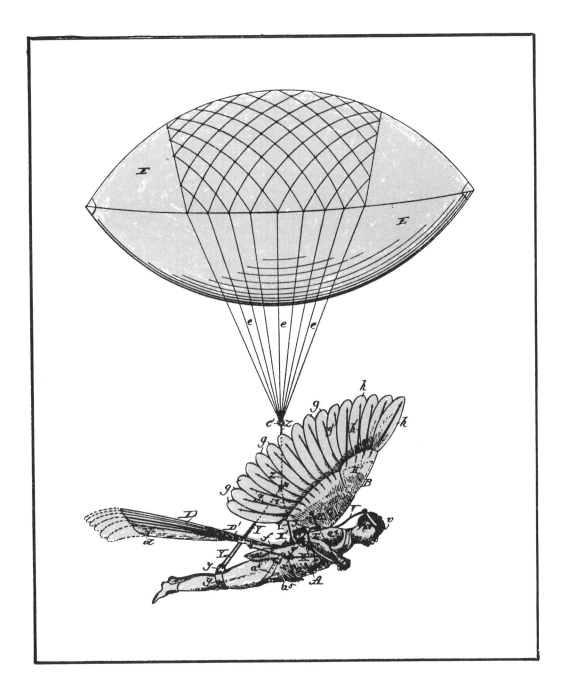

This drawing is from an application for a U.S. government patent. All those numbers and letters refer to materials and sizes for different parts of this flying apparatus. The drawing shows the sort of balloon that was to be used with the wings. The balloon would keep the flier up in the air and he would propel himself forward by flapping the wings.

FLYING LIKE A BIRD

How nice it would be to fly!

Just spread your wings and off you go — way up high above hills and trees and meadows, above the clouds, soaring like an eagle, flying from one place to another in no time at all.

Many people long ago had ideas like this. Wouldn't it be great, they thought. There are many old stories about attempts to fly.

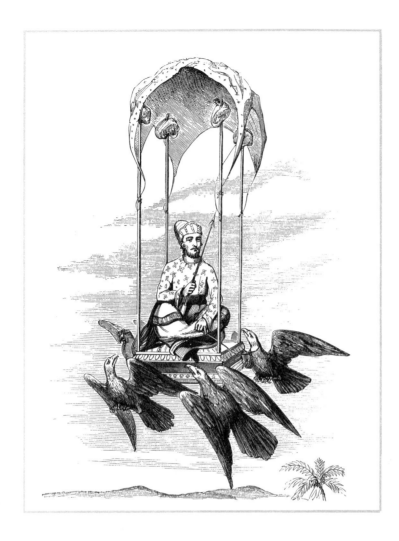

Here is an old engraving showing King Kavus carried aloft by his team of hungry eagles.

There is a fable about a certain King Kavus of Persia. He wanted to fly up into the heavens. What could be better for a king of Persia than a bird-drawn flying throne! And he had a plan. First, he had to find four strong eagles, very strong eagles. Then, he would attach a pole to each corner of his throne. There would be some tempting food fastened to the top of the poles. The eagles would be tied at the bottom of these poles. When the eagles got hungry, they would try to fly up to get at the food. This action would lift the throne and, of course, the king would be sitting there. Up they would go into the sky. When the birds grew tired, however, this aircraft would no doubt make a very bumpy landing.

There is another famous story about flying . . . a sad story. It is the legend of Icarus. It tells of Icarus and his father Daedalus. Daedalus made a set of wings for himself and another set of wings for his son so that they could fly away from a place where they were imprisoned. Daedalus told his son not to fly too high. "The sun will melt the wax that holds the feathers in place," he said.

But Icarus didn't heed his father. He flew too high, too close to the sun. The wax melted. The wings collapsed and Icarus fell into the sea and drowned.

Icarus fell to his death as his wings collapsed.

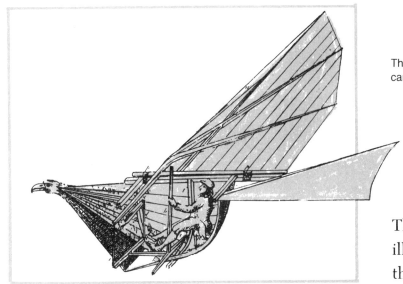

The idea for this unlikely flying machine came from watching the motion of birds' wings.

There are many legends and ancient illustrations of all sorts of flying things — winged horses, flying chariots, angels, magic carpets, and dragons with wings. By and by, many people began to think that a human being flying about in the sky might actually be possible.

The flying throne of King Kavus might not have been such a practical idea. But if a horse could pull a wagon along the ground, why couldn't a flock of birds pull some kind of air chair through the sky as shown below. To some people this seemed like a reasonable question.

Four eagles might not have been enough to carry King Kavus very far, but nine swans — or were they pigeons — might be able to carry this gentleman. In this old engraving, the birds are working hard and a little extra help is obtained from a small sail.

If you are going to design an aircraft, you might as well do it with style and with all the extras. This balloon, complete with giant rooster on top, has just about everything anybody could want. Drawings like this were much admired during the eighteenth century. Of course, such a flying machine was never built.

Nobody seems to have considered raising super large pigeons that could be ridden like horses. Instead of traveling by horseback, people could make much better time and avoid rocks, mud, forest, and mountains by traveling PIGEONBACK!

Many bright minds wrestled with the challenge of flight. Leonardo da Vinci, a great artist as well as an engineer and an inventor, came up with a plan for a flight machine as shown in the drawing opposite. A hard-working aviator is shown operating some ropes and pulleys to flap four wings.

Birds as a source of power was not the only idea considered. The machine shown here is something a mechanic might have dreamed up. All the little propellers were turned by hand and foot cranks but would probably do little more than raise clouds of dirt and dust.

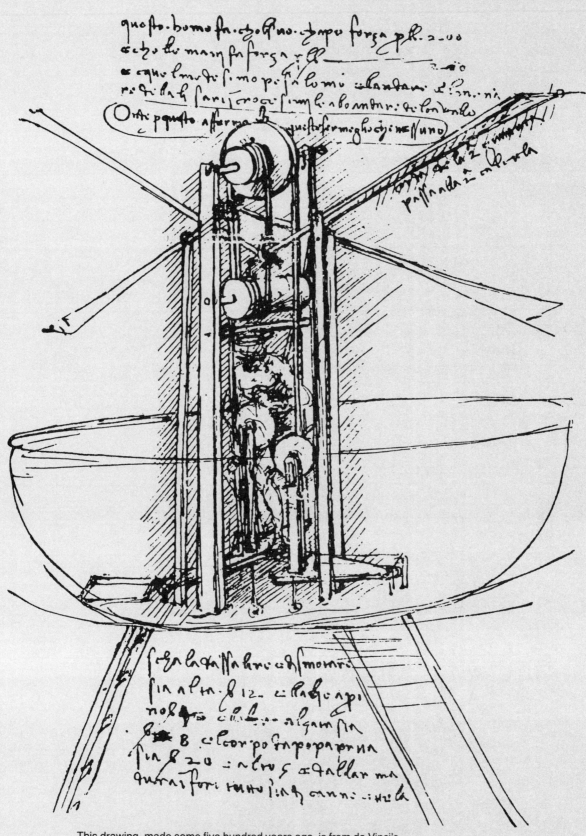

This drawing, made some five hundred years ago, is from da Vinci's sketchbook. It shows a complicated arrangement of pulleys and levers that would flap four winglike shapes to get this aircraft up into the air. The writing on the drawing can't be easily read because it is backward in an old Italian script. Da Vinci didn't want anyone reading and copying his ideas.

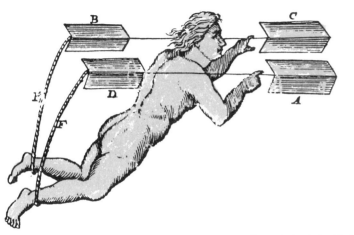

This fellow is using small, flapping wings that are worked by the feet as well as the hands. This drawing was made in 1678. (Evidently the artist who drew the picture thought it wasn't necessary to be very well dressed — or dressed at all — to operate this flying machine.) The small wing flaps at the end of the rods were supposed to close on the upstroke and open on the downstroke. The inventor of this aircraft, a French locksmith named P. Besnier, claimed in 1678 that he had jumped out of a window and flown over a barn. But nobody believed him!

FLAPPING WINGS

Most of the pioneers of flying spent a lot of time watching birds. They might say, "I'm surely smarter than a bird. If a bird can fly, why can't I?" They thought that if they could build a set of wings like a bird, they would fly like a bird. This sounds good — but unfortunately it won't work. A bird has a lightweight skeleton. Its muscles are intended to flap the wings, not to help the bird walk or run or lift heavy weights. And the wings themselves are constructed in ways that no human can copy.

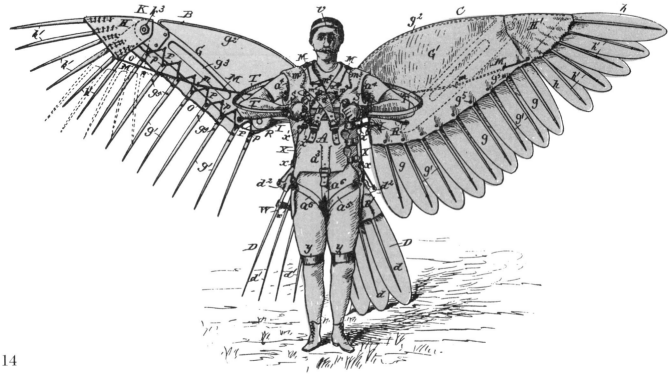

However, for a long time nobody understood this. All sorts of mechanical wings were built and attached to the body with straps and ropes and complicated harnesses. Many brave souls buckled on the wings and proceeded to jump off high places, expecting to sail away. These people were called *tower jumpers* because they took off from church towers, castle turrets, or any convenient high place. This was certainly the bravest kind of experimenting. But the flying in most cases was straight down . . . THUD! There were lots of bumps on the head, broken bones, and in some cases sudden deaths.

The illustration on the right is from a book on flying printed many years ago. However, the gentleman shown here doesn't seem to be in any danger. He looks as if he has jumped off this tower with the help of a rather strange-looking parachute.

38 HOMO VOLANS

◀ This clumsy and heavy-looking arrangement would perhaps have a hard time getting off the ground. Lightweight materials and streamlined shapes were unknown to early would-be fliers.

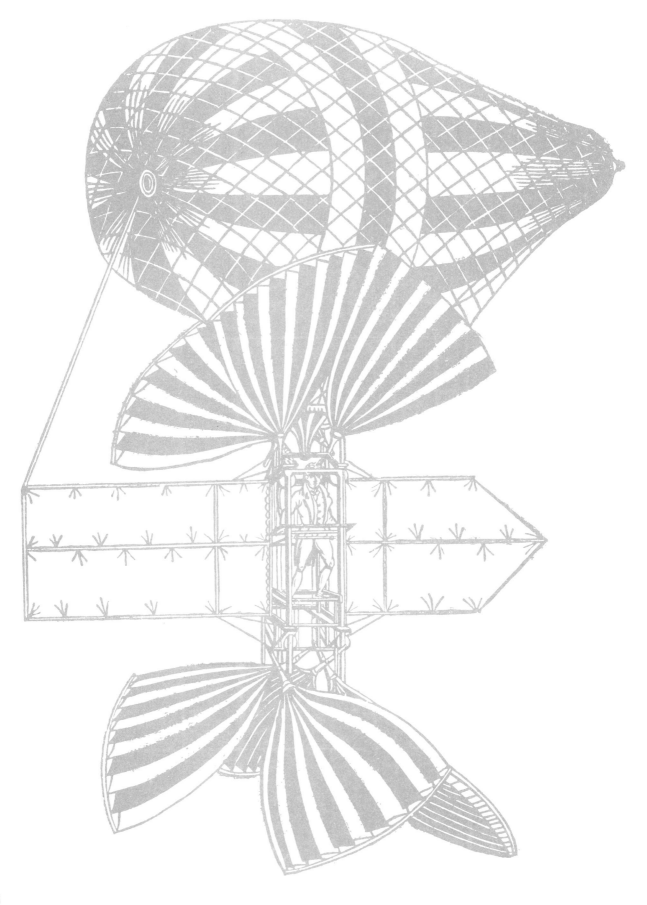

Often plans for flapping-wing aircraft were better works of art than practical, workable ideas. The rather complicated arrangement opposite makes a good-looking design but isn't likely to work. The odd-shaped balloon on top might be of some use, but there is a terrible tangle of big wing and sail shapes. The lone pilot in the center — in a sort of cage — would have quite a time trying to operate this contraption. But anyhow, most people would agree that it does make a nice picture!

Many eager beginners had ambitious ideas about flying but knew little about practical matters. The results were often as far-fetched as in this drawing.

Some artists think that most aircraft are things of beauty and good reason for taking pen or pencil in hand to make drawings that can be imaginative and attractive — even when the designs are not very practical. That is the case with the drawing below. It is by an artist who doesn't know too much about aircraft engineering and doesn't really care if these elaborate designs ever produce aircraft that fly. He just had fun making the drawing!

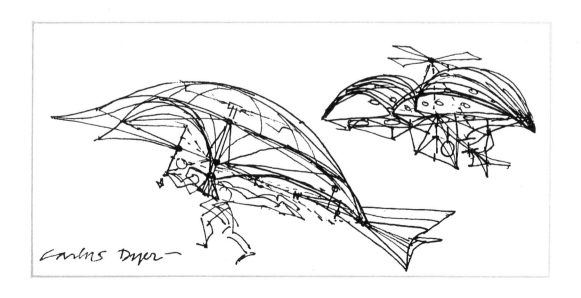

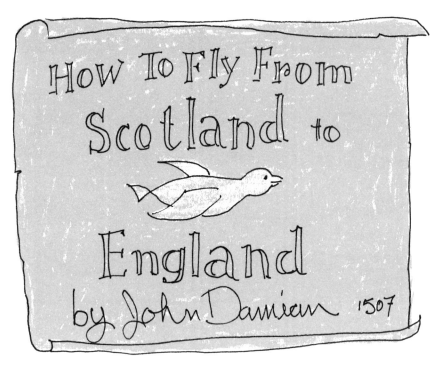

This is how Mr. John Damian's flight might have been described by one of his friends.

There is an account of a brave soul by the name of John Damian, who in 1507 thought he had designed a workable set of wings. He was so confident he announced for all to hear that he was going to fly from Scotland to England.

When the time came for the big flight, he climbed a high wall of a castle in Scotland. (He was a tower jumper.) He spread the wings, gave a mighty jump, flapped off, one might say, and — oops! — landed on a dunghill at the castle's base. He not only lost his dignity, he broke his leg.

But Damian wasn't about to admit failure. He said he had made a slight mistake in the choice of materials. He had used chicken feathers in the wings. Chickens are not much good as fliers, as everybody knows. But with eagle feathers, he declared he would be in London in no time at all. His broken leg eventually mended, but he never did try this flight again.

1. *Lots of feathers are needed — the more, the better.*

2. *The feathers must be carefully attached to the wing frame.*

3. *There are plenty of tall towers in Scotland that are good for jumping.*

4. *Luckily, only a leg was broken. "One day I'll try again!" he said.*

FLOATING ABOUT IN THE AIR — BALLOONS

It eventually occurred to some people that flapping wings
was not the best way to get up off the ground. Could it be
that there was a way to *float* up above the earth?

As early as 1670 a certain Father Francesco de Lana, an

Italian clergyman, thought up the flying machine shown on the opposite page. It is a very strange affair indeed. The good father reasoned that maybe a ball could be made that was light in weight and that had no air in it — a vacuum. It might be able to rise up through the surrounding air. You might compare this to a ball filled with air and submerged in water. Air weighs less than water so the ball will float upward. Likewise, a thin-walled ball filled with *nothing* would float up through air!

This sounds like a practical idea. But there were some serious problems that would keep it from working. The ball out of which the air was to be pumped would have to be very lightweight and, at the same time, strong enough to withstand the air pressure pushing in from all around it. Father de Lana planned to make the balls 20 feet in diameter, out of very thin copper foil. Unfortunately, the outside air pressure would have crushed them as soon as the air was pumped out.

Air is just as real as water, or earth, or any solid material even though you don't see it. Air has weight — and if it has

Here is a somewhat different version of Father de Lana's aircraft. It appeared in a book more than three hundred years ago. It shows three passengers. One is enjoying the ride while puffing away on a pipe. The pilot is steering with an oar and another passenger is clutching the mast and looking as though he is about to be seasick.

weight it can press on things. It produces pressure. Air has a pressure of 14.7 pounds per square inch. It is like a one-inch-square thumb pressing down with a force of 14.7 pounds! (We are surrounded by this kind of pressure at all times. The reason we don't feel it is that the pressure is at work all over, both inside and out.)

There is an experiment that proves air has weight: If all the air is removed from a bottle and the bottle is sealed, it will have a certain weight. Now, if the bottle is opened and weighed again, it will be found to weigh more! The air that has replaced the vacuum is the added weight. The fact that air has weight is very important to balloonists and aircraft builders.

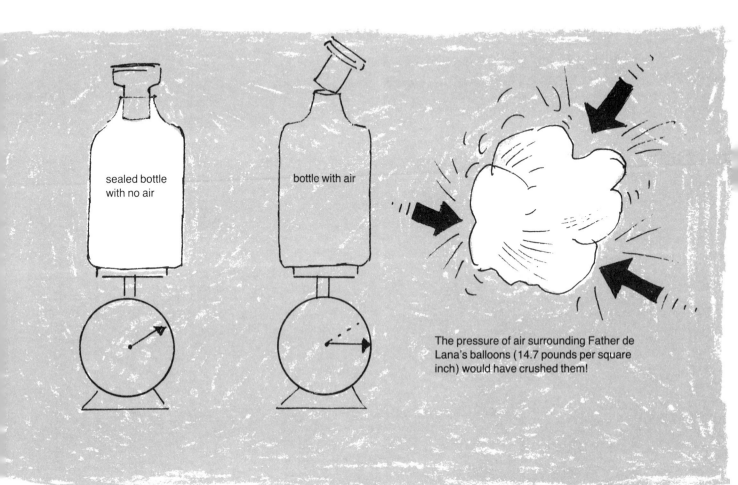

sealed bottle with no air

bottle with air

The pressure of air surrounding Father de Lana's balloons (14.7 pounds per square inch) would have crushed them!

Father de Lana's airship — a group of balloons with boat attached — was, of course, never built, even though it looked good on paper. But about one hundred years later in France the first lighter-than-air balloon did actually get off the ground.

The heated air inside the first hot air balloon wasn't like a vacuum. But, because the air was hot, it was lighter than the surrounding air. So, like a ball in water, the balloon floated upward.

Two brothers, Joseph and Etienne Montgolfier, had experimented with paper bags filled with hot air. They found that if the bag was light enough, and if there was enough heat, the bag would rise off the ground. The hot air inside the balloon was lighter than the surrounding air, so the balloon floated upward.

In 1783 they built a huge silk balloon that was lined with paper. It went for its first brief flight while still attached to the ground by ropes. The brothers weren't taking any chance of the balloon escaping! The first passengers were a sheep, a rooster, and a duck. When no harm came to them, a later flight took off with two brave human passengers.

This first free flight was over Paris. The balloon drifted about over the city for 25 minutes, then made a gentle, safe landing 5 miles away.

People came from near and far to see these first balloon flights. The idea of human beings drifting about in the sky, high overhead, was hard to believe. (In actual fact the very first flight with the sheep, rooster, and duck was not without accident. It was reported that the sheep kicked the rooster and broke its wing!)

This large and fancy balloon was built and flown in England shortly after the first flight of the Montgolfier balloon. There seems to be no fire to produce the hot air needed to keep it aloft, so the balloon must have been filled with lighter-than-air hydrogen gas.

The king of France, Louis XVI, watched the first flight. He was much impressed and said this might be a novel way to dispose of convicts. It must have seemed to him a good way to replace the guillotine.

These early flights were written about and illustrated in many of the journals of the day and captured the interest of scientists, inventors, and adventurers everywhere. When hydrogen gas was invented, it became possible to do away with fires that heated the air inside the balloon. Hydrogen was lighter than air and took the place of heated air. Balloons filled with hydrogen were sealed tight to keep the gas inside. Balloons using hot air, however, were open at the bottom so that the air could be heated.

The people who lived in the large towns and cities soon got used to seeing balloons drifting about in the sky. However, peasants on distant farms were alarmed when, for the first time, a strange balloon monster appeared. When it landed it was immediately attacked. The local farmers were taking no chances with this peculiar creature and they beat it fiercely, showing it no mercy at all.

Balloons go where they want to go. They float about at the whim of the wind. If the wind blows from the south, the balloon floats to the north. If it is an east wind, the balloon heads west. If there is no wind at all, the balloon just hovers, going no place.

For a time, floating in a balloon was great sport. Many stylish noblemen and women thought it great fun to drift about, getting nowhere when the wind wasn't blowing, but enjoying a fancy lunch with champagne, caviar, and dainty chicken sandwiches. What fun!

Today these simple balloons, using hot air rather than hydrogen or helium gas, and not very different from the original Montgolfier balloon, are still around. Some of these balloons have traveled long distances. They have floated across the Swiss Alps and there have been several attempts to fly them across the Atlantic Ocean. The hot air balloons of today don't use anything as clumsy and dangerous as burning straw and wood to produce the hot air. Instead, an efficient propane burner generates a quick heat that will rapidly inflate the balloon and keep it filled with hot air.

Because the hot air balloon is always without power and goes where the wind wants, it isn't a practical means of transportation.

But it was not long before the balloonists decided they wanted to go where they wanted, rather than where the wind wanted. So, a lot of thought was given to ways of moving and steering the balloon.

Here is one way of getting a balloon to go where you want it to go. The French inventor who thought up this idea was probably dreaming of something like an airborne horse and wagon. However, instead of a wagon, there is a sort of canoe. And instead of a horse, there is a gigantic bird.

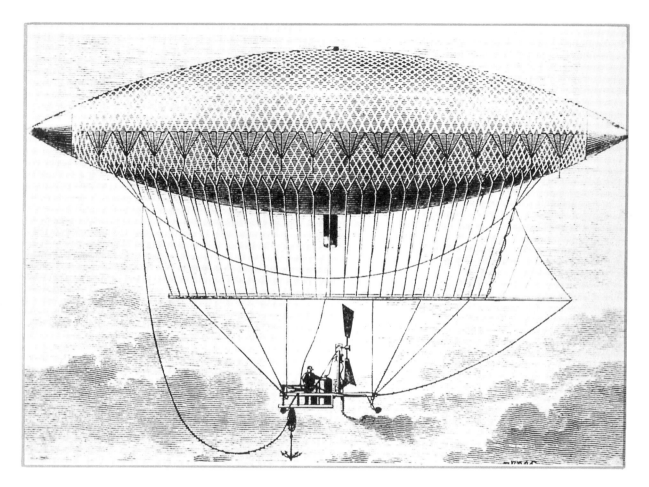

This balloon flying in Paris in 1852 used a steam engine to turn a large propeller. When a balloon is shaped like this and is large, has power and a way to steer, it is often called a *dirigible.* If it is small, it is sometimes called a *blimp* and can be seen occasionally carrying advertising messages on its sides. Notice the anchor hanging down ready for use when landing or in an emergency.

Everything from oars to paddles to massive steam engines were tried in order to move the balloon in a planned direction. Some of these ideas were fanciful indeed, like the big bird pulling the boat on the opposite page. Notice the two labels in French in this illustration. ***Force Ascensionnelle*** above the balloon refers to the force needed to ascend, or rise. ***Force Directrice*** means the force required to get this aircraft moving in the desired direction. All that was needed to make this scheme work was the right bird!

This much improved balloon was photographed in the early 1900s. There is a large rudder to make steering easy. Behind the pilot is a small gasoline engine. If you look carefully, you can see the long shaft that goes from the engine to the propeller, which is just in front of the rudder.

Once hydrogen was available balloons became larger and were differently shaped. Now they could carry heavy engines to turn the propellers. These balloons could go where the balloonists wanted, not where the winds wanted them to go.

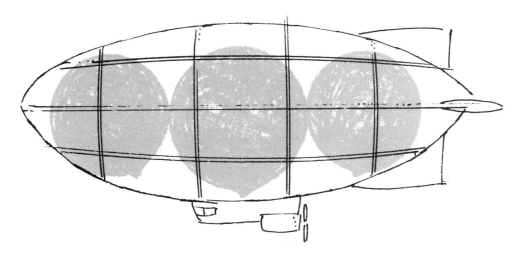

Large dirigibles were built as shown in this drawing. Many large gas bags were held within a lightweight metal framework. The engines were suspended from this framework as well as cabins for passengers and crew.

The *Hindenburg,* a huge dirigible, built some fifty years ago, had flown back and forth between Germany and America many times with no problems. But, on its last trip in 1937, it exploded violently as it approached its mooring tower in New Jersey. Thirty-four passengers and crew members were killed. Nobody knows what caused the explosion, but hydrogen was being used to keep the airship aloft. The accident wouldn't have occurred if nonexplosive helium had been used. Helium, a lighter-than-air gas, is in general use today.

GETTING PRACTICAL

Eventually would-be fliers gave up ideas about
bird-propelled aircraft or strap-on wings. Balloons were
fine in their own way, but they didn't really *fly!* So, people
began to look not only at birds, but at different kinds of
kites. After all, a kite flies even though it is tied to the
ground by a thin string. They reasoned that it must be the
action of the wind flowing against the kite that kept it up in
the air.

The study of air as it flows against and around various objects is called *aerodynamics.* It is a very important scientific field that deals with the shape and performance of all sorts of things that pass through air — from aircraft, to trucks, to locomotives, to ballistic missiles.

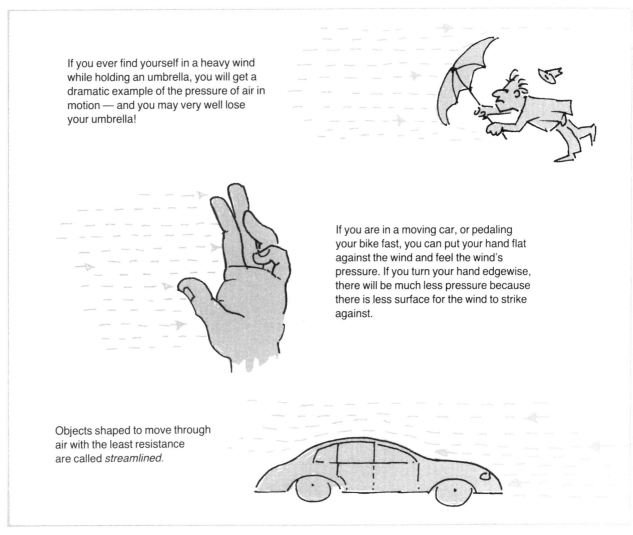

If you ever find yourself in a heavy wind while holding an umbrella, you will get a dramatic example of the pressure of air in motion — and you may very well lose your umbrella!

If you are in a moving car, or pedaling your bike fast, you can put your hand flat against the wind and feel the wind's pressure. If you turn your hand edgewise, there will be much less pressure because there is less surface for the wind to strike against.

Objects shaped to move through air with the least resistance are called *streamlined.*

Curious inventors and scientists eventually began to think about the size and shape of wings — bird and kite wings. And this led to the notion of the glider. The wings on some gliders may look like kites, or the flapping wings of the tower jumpers, but they are different. Flapping wings just beat against the air without doing much, except raise a lot of dust. The wings on a glider or most other modern aircraft don't flap. They are firmly attached in place. The fixed wing of a glider is not unlike a kite, and it uses the pressure and the flow of air to get a lifting motion.

Many different kinds of wings were tried on both model and full-scale gliders. These first gliders were a fine way to experiment with a variety of wing shapes. A great deal was learned and led eventually to practical flight.

One of the first people to deal with wings in a scientific way was an Englishman by the name of George Cayley, who lived in the early 1800s. He said that flapping wings were fine for birds, but for people to fly, fixed wings were needed. He experimented to find the best glider-wing angle. A curved wing, he learned, was more efficient than a straight, flat wing and a tail was needed for stability. The

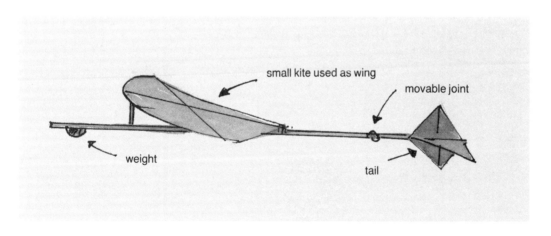

Sir George Cayley's model glider, built in 1804, doesn't look like much, but at the time it was an important step towards the beginning of practical air flight. It had a movable joint so that the tail could be adjusted. The wing was from a kite. A small weight was used for balance, and the body of this aircraft was a simple stick.

model glider that he built had an adjustable tail. It was not like the model planes that people have these days. But, it was the first practical, working-model aircraft.

Sir George Cayley also designed and built another full-size glider. It was known as a Boy Glider because a ten-year-old boy went for several short test flights on it. History doesn't tell us the name of this boy pilot, but he must have been a brave young man. Or, maybe he was NOT brave enough to say to Sir George, "No sir, not me. I'm not going to break my neck in that contraption!"

The Boy Glider had three wings and two tails as well as a pair of small oars on the side. The oars were supposed to row the glider through the air once it was in flight. Unfortunately, the glider never rose more than a few feet off the ground for a second or two, and the boy didn't get much of a ride other than a fast trundle down a long slope.

You might want to experiment yourself with a very simple model aircraft a little like Sir George Cayley's. All you need is a stick, a rubber band, some stiff paper, a couple of coins, and some tape. Your finished product won't be exactly like Sir George's — but it will fly. Assemble the glider as shown. Then try it out where you have lots of room, out of doors, if possible. Try holding the plane in different positions, as you gently launch it. Fuss with it until it flies the way you want.

The most important part of this model is the stick. It should be square — ¼″ by ¼″ — and 11″ long. Balsa wood, which is very light, is best for this model, but you can get by with most any kind of wood. The wings should be of strong paper, about the weight of a heavy post card. If you cut up an empty breakfast cereal box, you will have just the thing.

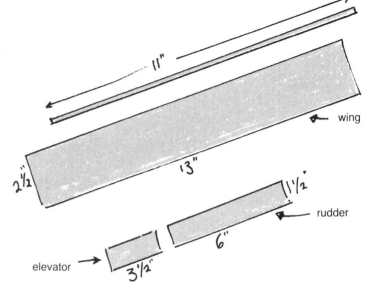

The tail should be made of lighter paper than the wing. A file folder or lightweight post card will provide what you need. You can use glue to hold rudder and stabilizer in place.

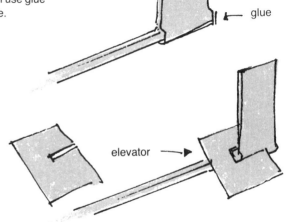

In order to get a small glider like this to fly properly, you will have to be like Sir George Cayley and do a lot of adjusting, changing, and general fussing around. It would be unusual for your glider to fly nicely the first time you launch it!

Try moving the wing forward or backward along the stick. See if you get a better flight with the wings bent slightly up. If your plane wants to dive downward, see if a lighter nose weight will help. If the nose goes up, add more weight, or try moving the wing back a little.

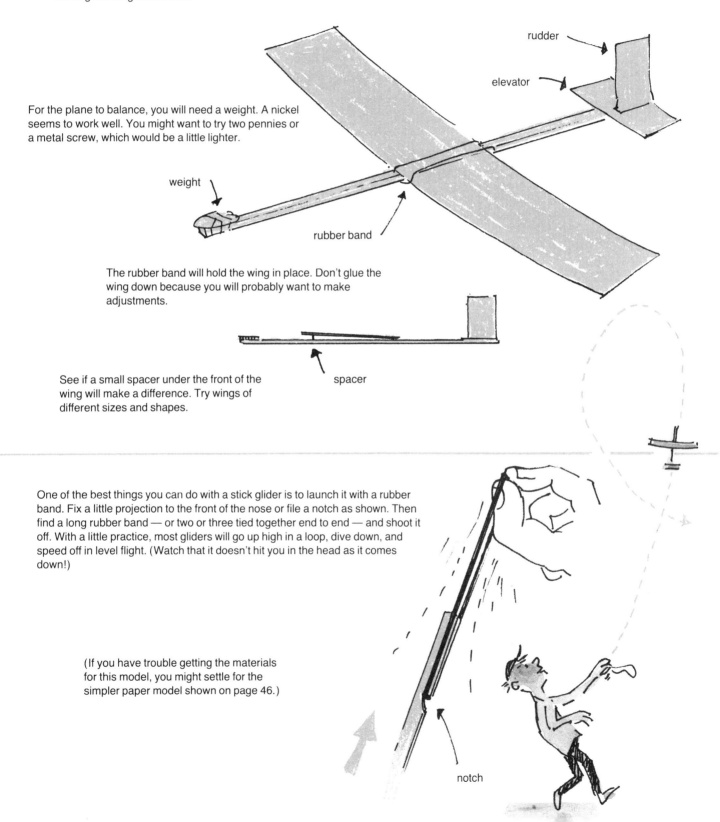

rudder

elevator

For the plane to balance, you will need a weight. A nickel seems to work well. You might want to try two pennies or a metal screw, which would be a little lighter.

weight

rubber band

The rubber band will hold the wing in place. Don't glue the wing down because you will probably want to make adjustments.

See if a small spacer under the front of the wing will make a difference. Try wings of different sizes and shapes.

spacer

One of the best things you can do with a stick glider is to launch it with a rubber band. Fix a little projection to the front of the nose or file a notch as shown. Then find a long rubber band — or two or three tied together end to end — and shoot it off. With a little practice, most gliders will go up high in a loop, dive down, and speed off in level flight. (Watch that it doesn't hit you in the head as it comes down!)

(If you have trouble getting the materials for this model, you might settle for the simpler paper model shown on page 46.)

notch

A famous experimenter with gliders was a German named Otto Lilienthal. He built all kinds of gliders in the 1890s, just a few years before the Wright brothers started to build their gliders. Lilienthal built a rather large hill for testing his gliders. Then he could jump off in any direction, facing the wind. A few of his gliders look a little like the hang gliders that are flown nowadays by would-be aviators.

This is a photograph of Otto Lilienthal sailing along on one of his first gliders.

Lilienthal was trained as an engineer. But even before that, as a young boy, he spent much of his time studying the flight of birds. He found the stork especially interesting. He decided that the way the surface of the wing was curved had a lot to do with the bird's ability to glide through the air. He also gave a lot of thought to how birds managed to soar on rising air currents.

The great artist Leonardo da Vinci had ideas somewhat like Lilienthal's about four hundred years earlier. The drawing of a wing shape on the opposite page is from one of da Vinci's sketchbooks. An actual model of this design, however, was never built.

Lilienthal had this to say more than a hundred years ago about glider flying: "The feat of launching by running down a slope into the wind until sufficient velocity is reached to lift the operator and his forty-pound wings requires practice. In the beginning the height should be moderate and the wings not too large for the wind will show that it is not to be trifled with. To those who have gained full control of the apparatus, it is not in the least dangerous to cross deep and broad ravines."

Even though this sounds like a safe and not-too-demanding way of traveling, it turned out quite differently for Lilienthal. He took off from a hill one breezy day in 1896 for what was to be his last flight. A sudden gust of wind thrust his glider upward and it stalled. He shifted his weight to try and get the glider back in balance, but he couldn't manage it. The left wing dipped and the glider, out of control, plunged to the ground. Lilienthal, his back broken, died the next day. This was not the first, nor certainly the last, of many air tragedies.

This drawing by Leonardo da Vinci shows a wing design not unlike some of Lilienthal's.

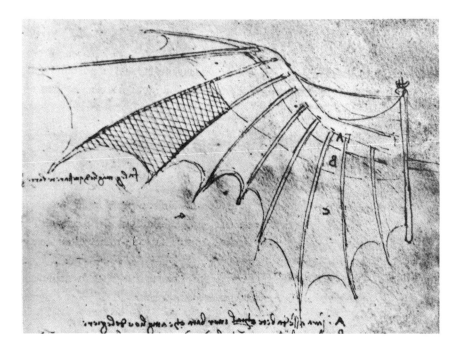

Here is Lilienthal in one of his more ambitious gliders. It is a *biplane* glider, which means it has two wings — an upper and a lower wing. There is also a fairly elaborate tail. With no way to steer the glider, it had to be controlled by shifting one's weight. This demanded some strong and energetic work.

Gliders are still used today, but they are quite different. There are large, sleek gliders that are towed up high by powered airplanes. Then they are cut loose and allowed to sail about on their own. When the conditions are right a skilled glider pilot can soar for many hours, skimming along from one rising air current to another. And there are also the smaller hang gliders often seen sailing off hillsides on breezy days.

Modern gliders look like fast, powered airplanes. Only the engine is missing.

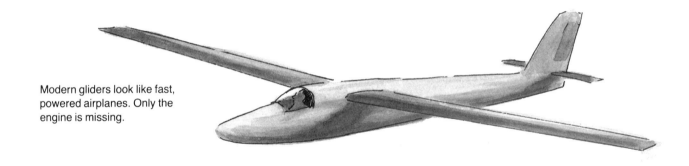

More than one would-be flier decided that a large wing mounted on a bicycle would make a sure-to-fly glider.

The hang gliders, which are very popular with some adventurous young people, look a little like the gliders that were experimented with a hundred or more years ago. Actually they are not the same. The shape of the wing is quite different. In most cases there are no rigid frames like Lilienthal's. The modern hang glider is made from materials that didn't exist many years ago. Nylon or Dacron is used for the wing instead of silk or cotton. Just a few lightweight aluminum poles and thin, strong, stainless-steel wire provide the support for the wing.

Flying a hang glider requires an athletic body, training, and sometimes a good deal of courage.

WHAT KEEPS IT UP?

Aircraft are always fighting a battle against gravity, the force that pulls everything towards the center of the earth. There are two forces at work that let aircraft with wings win the battle against gravity.

One is the force of wind pressure pushing against the underside of the wing. This is the same as the air pressing against kites and gliders. The other is the sucking force caused by the air flowing along the upper side of a curved wing. Because the air moves faster along the curved, top surface of the wing, the pressure is reduced here, and the wing is pulled up. A scientific principle states that pressure is reduced when fluid or air passes at an increased speed over a surface. It is called the *Bernoulli principle*, named after a Swiss scientist who lived in the eighteenth century.

These forces are at work only while the aircraft is moving and the air is moving rapidly over and under the surface of the wing.

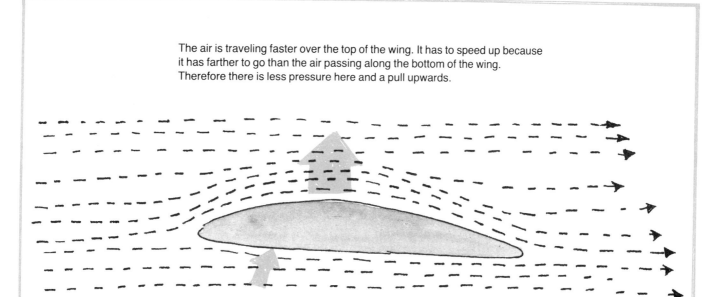

The air is traveling faster over the top of the wing. It has to speed up because it has farther to go than the air passing along the bottom of the wing. Therefore there is less pressure here and a pull upwards.

Air is also pushing up against the underside of the wing.

In modern aircraft the position and the shape of the wing are carefully planned in order to get the most lift. *Lift* refers to the upward forces that act on an airplane. It is the force that opposes gravity and keeps an aircraft up in the air.

The forces that are at work on a glider wing are at work on all kinds of aircraft. The wing on a hang glider, even if it is made of only thin cloth, is operating in basically the same way as the wing on a supersonic jet fighter plane.

There are some times, however, when the action of air on wings is not considered. And that, of course, is when there are no wings! This is the case with rockets or spacecraft, where an entirely different set of conditions has to be dealt with.

USING POWER

By the end of the 1800s many scientists and engineers were getting close to building a practical aircraft. Quite a few model airplanes had been constructed that flew fairly well. It was just a question of time until a full-scale aircraft would be built. One bright French scientist by the name of Alphonse Pénaud made some ingenious model planes propelled by rubber bands. These were *powered* models.

The rubber band is something we take for granted today. We are familiar with its many uses. But, it was a big discovery in 1870, when one was twisted up tight and then allowed to untwist in order to turn a propeller. A great deal was learned from experiments with models like these.

Most hobby or toy stores sell simple airplane kits using balsa wood. In a short time — and without much effort — you can build a model not unlike Pénaud's. (The

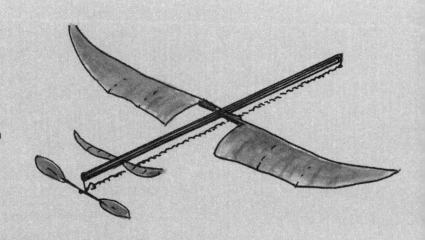

This is Pénaud's twisted rubber band–propelled model. The wings were not perfectly flat, but slightly curved in the shape that had proved most effective. The propeller in this model is at the rear in what is called a pusher arrangement.

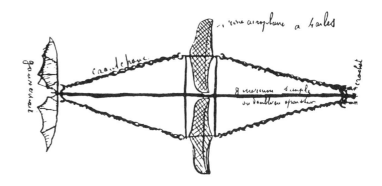

This drawing by Alphonse Pénaud is for an odd-looking, powered aircraft using two small wings turned by twisted rubber bands. There are two sets of rubber bands for each wing. It is not known if this model was ever built or if it would work.

propeller will be in front, however, not like Pénaud's.) These kits are complete with propeller, right-size rubber band "engine," wheels, and all the other parts you'll need. The simple kits are inexpensive, although large, complicated kits that will make large-scale aircraft are available.

The rubber band–powered models that have wheels are able to take off from the ground. They will roll along on any smooth surface, then soar into the air and keep flying as long as the rubber band is unwinding. Then they will gracefully glide to a smooth landing. However, any glider or powered model plane will not do well if there is a strong wind or rain or drizzle. It is also important to do your flying in an open area — away from trees, power lines, and underbrush.

This is a typical airplane model built from an easily assembled kit.

If you can't get a rubber band–powered kit from a store or find the materials to build a stick glider, and if you still have an urge to make some kind of aircraft, you can make a simple little glider like the one shown here. All you need is a sheet of 8½-by-11-inch paper and a few pieces of tape.

1. Make a crease along the center line. Lay the paper down on a flat surface.
2. Fold in the corners along the dotted lines.
3. Fold again on the dotted lines.
4. This is how your glider should look now.
5. Fold along the original crease that you made in step 1. (Fold so that the wings are down and the center crease is up.) Then lay the paper on its side and carefully fold along the dotted line on both sides to get the wings.
6. Put a piece of tape on top and on bottom to keep the wings from spreading apart and you are ready to go. If after adjusting, your glider doesn't fly the way you like, get another piece of paper and try again.

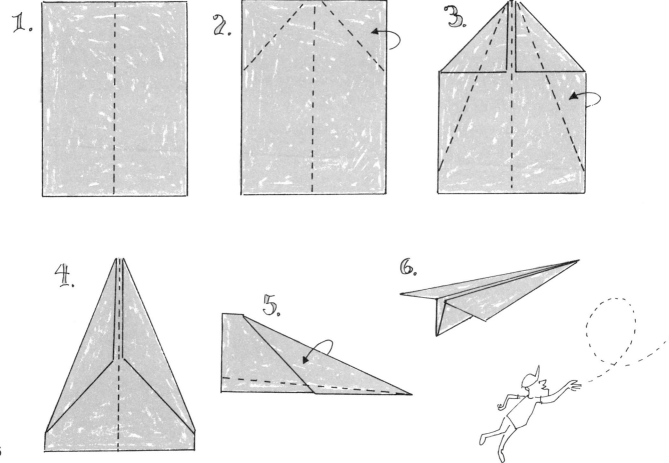

46

In the late 1800s everything seemed ready for the development of a practical, working airplane. Hot air and gas balloons were often seen floating over American and European cities. Some were fitted with engines and could travel in any direction. But there were no airplanes to be seen. There had been many experiments with gliders, and a good deal was known about wing shapes and the principles of flight. The next step was to put together all this knowledge and experience. And that meant fitting a lightweight engine onto a strong glider body. If this could be done there would finally be a powered, fixed-wing aircraft!

There were many attempts to build this kind of flying machine. Some of these efforts seem very strange. But quite a few ideas were useful and not too different from designs used in modern aircraft. If a lightweight, efficient engine had been available at this time, practical flight would have been possible.

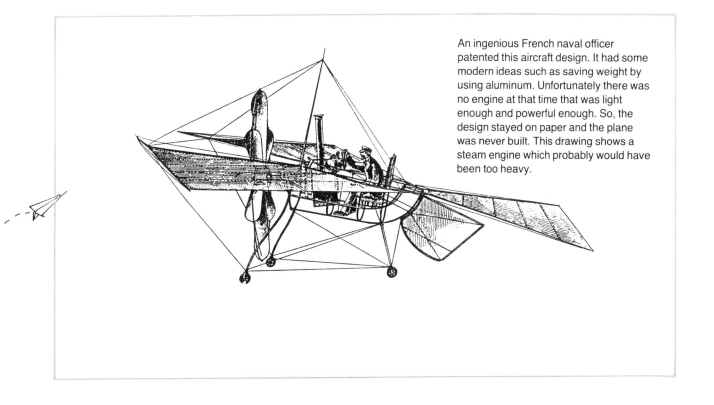

An ingenious French naval officer patented this aircraft design. It had some modern ideas such as saving weight by using aluminum. Unfortunately there was no engine at that time that was light enough and powerful enough. So, the design stayed on paper and the plane was never built. This drawing shows a steam engine which probably would have been too heavy.

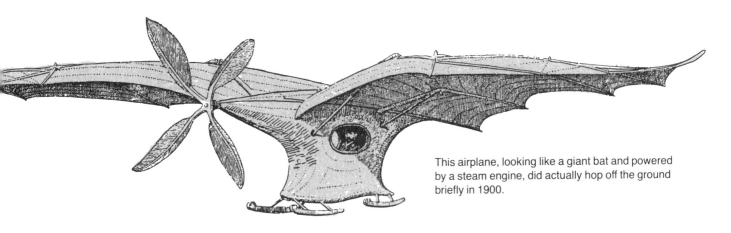

This airplane, looking like a giant bat and powered by a steam engine, did actually hop off the ground briefly in 1900.

Some of the first ideas for a flying machine were a little like helicopters. Leonardo da Vinci made a drawing that looked almost workable. He must have thought, If a screw can twist itself into wood, why can't a large screw twist itself up into the air? Actually a propeller is a sort of screw, and it *can* twist its way through the air.

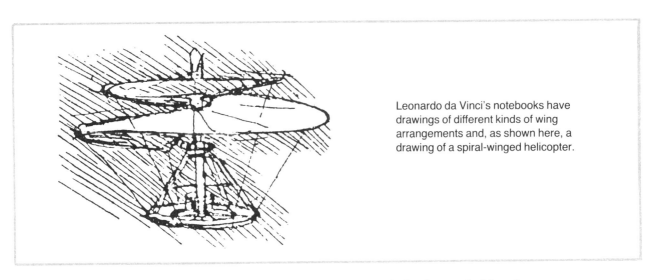

Leonardo da Vinci's notebooks have drawings of different kinds of wing arrangements and, as shown here, a drawing of a spiral-winged helicopter.

The propeller of a helicopter doesn't look much like the da Vinci screw-propeller, nor like the propeller used on a small plane. But it does work in much the same way.

Making a good propeller is actually a scientific undertaking, and the result has a lot to do with how well an aircraft works. In the beginning most propellers were

Many inventors and engineers tried hard to build a workable helicopter. This model, which was actually built, looks quite practical. The large, rotating blades seem simple enough. But the steam engine is a complicated affair with cylinders, heating coils, and boiler. It is a neat-looking machine but much too heavy to get off the ground.

simply twisted boards or big paddles. The first efficient propellers were designed by the Wright brothers for their own airplane.

Quite a few scientists tried to make a practical helicopter. The way propeller blades operate was understood. The difficulty was finding an engine that wouldn't be too heavy, yet was powerful enough to turn the propeller. All sorts of model helicopters were built during the 1800s. Most of them were operated by little steam engines. There were also toy helicopters built with rubber band engines that used feathers for wings.

Even though a flapping-wing aircraft was impractical, Pénaud couldn't resist the challenge to build a model that worked on this principle. (An aircraft like this with flapping wings is called an *ornithopter*.)

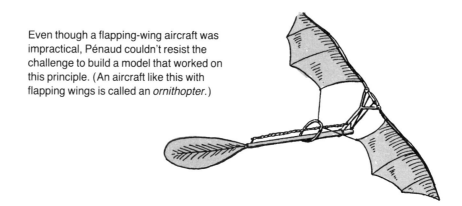

You can easily make a flying-propeller helicopter that is a lot of fun. It is just a plain propeller without the rest of the plane attached underneath! All you need to make it go is a piece of string and the strength of your arm.

It is not difficult to put together and it is quite a sight as the propeller goes spinning up high in the air. The one I've made goes up 20 feet or more, and I have to be careful not to get it stuck in the branches of the trees in my back yard.

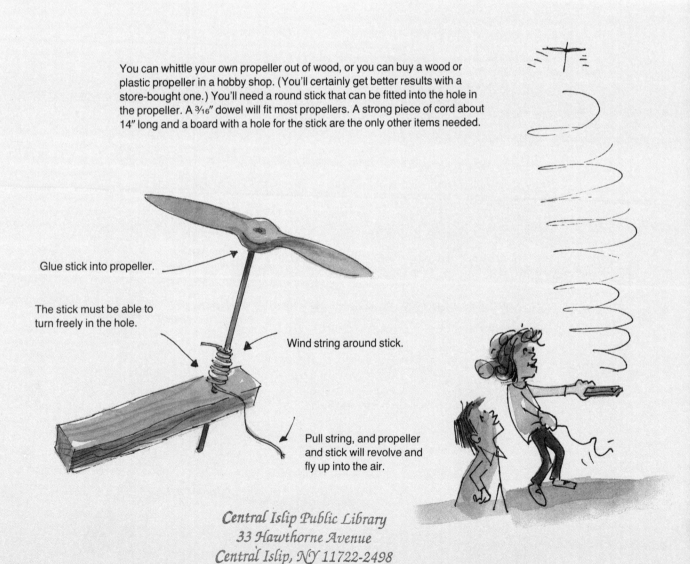

You can whittle your own propeller out of wood, or you can buy a wood or plastic propeller in a hobby shop. (You'll certainly get better results with a store-bought one.) You'll need a round stick that can be fitted into the hole in the propeller. A 3/16" dowel will fit most propellers. A strong piece of cord about 14" long and a board with a hole for the stick are the only other items needed.

Glue stick into propeller.

The stick must be able to turn freely in the hole.

Wind string around stick.

Pull string, and propeller and stick will revolve and fly up into the air.

Central Islip Public Library
33 Hawthorne Avenue
Central Islip, NY 11722-2498

TOIL AND TROUBLE

Most of the first trials and experiments with aircraft were anything but successful. All sorts of accidents and failures occurred. There is nothing surprising about this. As new inventions are developed, this is what usually happens. The Wright brothers, as well as most other inventors, had many problems to solve before they were successful.

Samuel Pierpont Langley, a scientist, was working at the same time as the Wright brothers to build a

The Langley aircraft can be seen here perched on a barge floating on the Potomac River. The barge had a catapult that was supposed to launch the airplane. A flight over this large stretch of water was intended to avoid trees or buildings that might get in the way of the flight. As it turned out, such precautions were not needed.

In this photo it is easy to see how the airplane was headed for trouble . . . headed down rather than up. It is unclear whether the faulty launch was because of trouble with the catapult or with the design of the airplane.

passenger-carrying airplane. Langley was an important man, the president of the Smithsonian Institution in Washington, D.C., and he was much experienced with technical matters.

He designed a large, carefully engineered aircraft that was launched off a river barge and went — *SPLASH!* — straight into the river. This aircraft had been designed after experiments with smaller models that worked quite well. If it wasn't for some bad luck on takeoff, this aircraft might very well have made the first successful manned flight. But the plane was broken up in its crash, and Langley was too discouraged to try again. The same year that Langley failed the Wright brothers made their historic flight at Kitty Hawk.

There were many accidents and crashes as different kinds of engines were combined with unsuitable, fragile aircraft bodies. Actually, the worst accidents during these times were with balloons. Several of them caught fire.

Others got into tangles with dangling ropes, broken controls, and sudden, violent storms. And more than a few balloonists were lost at sea when their craft took off in the wrong direction.

One particularly tragic balloon expedition ended with death in the far north. A Swedish engineer and two assistants set out in a large balloon on a voyage to the North Pole. They headed north for several days, everything seeming to go well. Then the balloon vanished! Disappeared. Nothing was heard of it for thirty-three years — until 1930, when a ship hunting for seals in arctic waters discovered the balloon wreck and the bodies of the three passengers. Photographs and notes in the logbook found with the bodies told about the last desperate days as the crew attempted to stay alive on the ice with little food or shelter.

THE WRIGHT BROTHERS

Two young bicycle mechanics named Orville and Wilbur
Wright became fascinated with the problems of flight just
a few years before 1900. While they were still children,
their father had given them a rubber band–powered model
plane. This is what first got them interested in flight. They
decided that aviation would be their lifework. At first they
supported themselves by making and selling bicycles, but
airplanes were what they really cared about.

    They started out by building gliders, which they flew

like kites. They spent a great deal of time experimenting with wing shapes and ways to control these glider-kites while in the air. Eventually they built larger gliders, like the ones shown on these pages, which could carry people. They flew these on the windy sand dunes of Kitty Hawk. The gliders had a wing shape that was the result of many trials and experiments. The wings could be twisted in order to control the direction of flight. The Wrights called this wing twisting *warping*. It enabled the pilot to steer the glider better.

On these first Wright aircraft, the elevator (in front) and the rudder (in back) were fixed in place. They helped steady the plane in flight. In modern airplanes the rudder

The Wright gliders were very light, fragile affairs. They were built with spruce wood and the wings were covered with finely woven cloth. A helping hand on each side got this glider off to a straight start.

Here is a close-up view of Orville in flight. You can see quite clearly the elevator in front and how it is held in place. In later, improved models the angle of the elevator could be altered for better control.

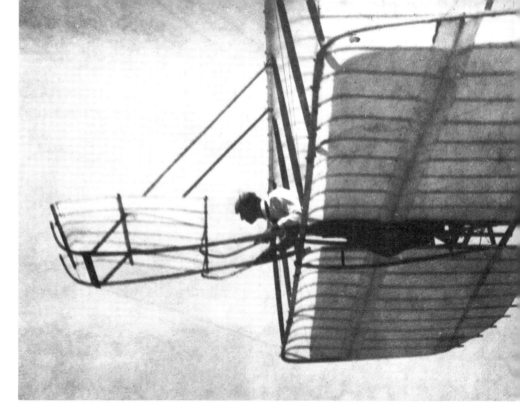

The Wrights chose Kitty Hawk for their flights because the winds were strong and steady there. However, a gust of wind could sometimes be too strong or from the wrong direction, causing a situation like this. The brothers had other reasons for choosing this location. There were no trees or buildings in the way. There were gentle sand dunes for launching, and the sand was less likely to cause damage from hard landings.

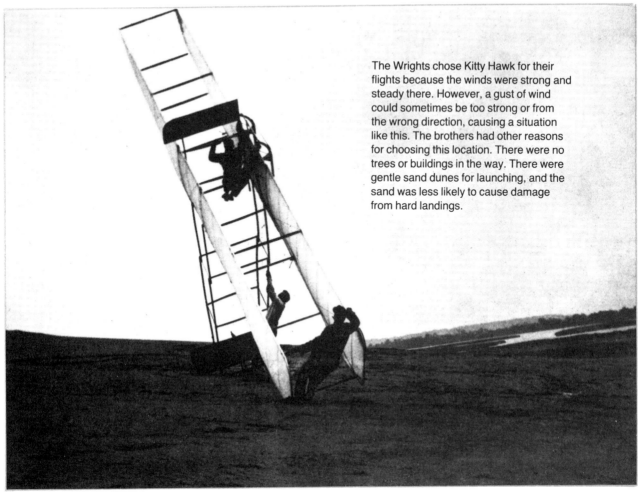

and the elevator, which are both in the tail, are movable and control direction.

After several years of continual changes and testing, the Wrights felt that they had the ideal unpowered aircraft. Now they needed the power.

The problem was to get a suitable engine. They tried to find an automobile engine that would work for them. Not one of these was just right, so they built their own. Their engine weighed 140 pounds and delivered 12 horsepower.

In 1903 the aircraft, with engine and two propellers, was finally put together and ready to go. The two brothers flipped a coin to see who would make the first flight. Wilbur won the toss. He raced the plane along the take-off track and it lifted a few feet into the air. Then it suddenly nosed down into the sand — crunch! Wilbur said the fault was his, not the plane's. He hadn't properly controlled the flight.

This is a famous photograph of the first powered flight of the Wright brothers' airplane, which was named *Flyer*. Orville is the pilot and Wilbur is running alongside.

A few days later, after repairs had been made, it was his brother's turn. This time a short but controlled flight was made. Orville had this to say: "It was the first time in the history of the world in which a machine carrying a man had raised itself by its own power into the air and in full flight had sailed forward without a reduction of power and had finally landed at a point as high as that from which it had started." This was the beginning of the age of flight!

Once the Wright brothers had made this first short airborne journey the doors were opened for practical flight. People all over the world realized that at last a passenger-carrying, powered aircraft was really possible. Most of the aircraft built at this time were based on the Wright brothers' designs, and looked like their *Flyer*. But gradually, with more experience and new ideas, the shapes began to change. Wheels were added to make landings a little smoother. Then different-shaped wings were tried. However, some of these first planes were strange indeed, and some were quite impractical.

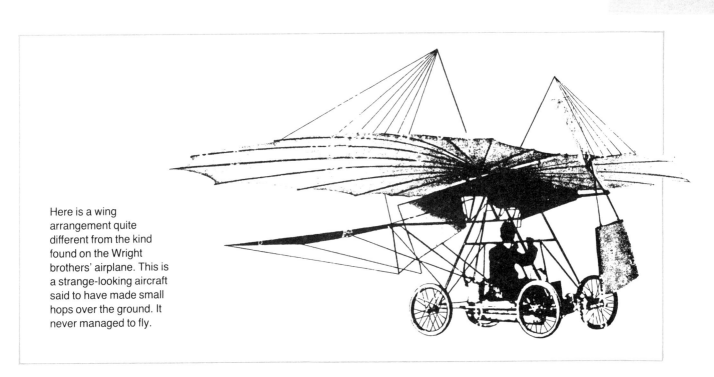

Here is a wing arrangement quite different from the kind found on the Wright brothers' airplane. This is a strange-looking aircraft said to have made small hops over the ground. It never managed to fly.

This plane was built by Glenn Curtiss some six years after the Wright brothers' first flight. As you can see, there are quite a few improvements. There are wheels to make landing easier. The pilot is seated, not lying down on the lower wing, and he is using a steering wheel. There is only one propeller, powered by a 50-horsepower gasoline engine. Another view of this plane, the *Golden Flier*, is on the title page of this book.

Planes with one wing — called *monoplanes* — were tried and worked quite well. Planes with three and even four wings were flown. And by the time of the First World War (1914–1918), airplanes of all types were seen everywhere. They became a safe and dependable way of traveling. In wartime they were used to drop bombs or shoot down other planes.

It seemed to some people that if one wing was good and two better, then three, four, or more wings would be still better. The airplane here had many very narrow wings. This was called the venetian blind style of wing design, and though it sounds reasonable, it never worked.

After the Wrights, it seemed as if all the world wanted to see how far, how fast, and how high an airplane could fly. Air meets of all kinds were organized in America and in Europe. This photograph shows a French flier by the name of Henri Farman winning a prize in 1908 by flying a circular course — a distance of 1 mile — in 1 minute, 28 seconds.

By 1910 airplanes could travel at what seemed amazing speeds. An airplane of this type set a speed record of 62 miles an hour. This monoplane is ready to go, with pilot sitting up where he can see what's going on. When the four ground crew let go, the plane will be off and away.

Eventually very large aircraft were built. Materials changed. Airplanes were constructed of lightweight aluminum instead of wood and cloth. There were planes that could carry hundreds of passengers or tons of cargo. Helicopters came into general use.

Jet engines replaced gasoline engines that turned propellers. Speeds beyond the speed of sound were possible. And, finally, there were aircraft that could travel to the moon and beyond, or simply hover in space in a permanent orbit, doing all kinds of useful tasks and scientific research.

The most modern "aircraft," like the one shown on the following page, is not really an aircraft at all. It travels in space where there is *no* air, so you can't honestly call it an aircraft.

It is a spacecraft and is launched by a huge rocket. The drawing is of the *Mariner II* which, several years ago, made a brief, passing visit to the planet Venus. It learned a good deal about this planet, although the spacecraft only came within several thousand miles of it. The two winglike shapes on the *Mariner II* are not wings at all. Wings would have no purpose where there is no air. They are solar panels that catch the sunlight and change it into the electricity that powers the *Mariner's* many instruments.

The *Mariner II* may not look much like an ordinary airplane, but it is the result of a long line of related discoveries, experiments, and research that began long before the Wright brothers'. Without the work of the pioneers of flight, there wouldn't be the sort of air and space travel that we have today.

MORE ABOUT EARLY AIRCRAFT

Many books, which can be found in most libraries, have been written about aviation and the history of flying. There are books about particular aspects of flying — gliders, rockets, ballooning, and modern aircraft — and about particular people, such as the Wright brothers, Charles Lindbergh, Amelia Earhart, and others.

There is one place that everybody who is interested in flying and aircraft would be very lucky to visit: the National Air and Space Museum in Washington, D.C. It is a huge building with all sorts of historically important aircraft — and spacecraft. You'll find there the Wright brothers' *Flyer*, Lindbergh's *Spirit of St. Louis*, World War II fighter planes, vehicles from space, and all sorts of fascinating models.

The National Air and Space Museum has published several books that have many photographs and tell about the museum's collection. If you can't get to the museum, the books are the next best thing.

A visit to your local airport is another thing that many people find exciting. You won't get to see any historic aircraft, but watching all sorts of modern planes land and take off, as well as seeing all the bustle and excitement there, can be great fun.

APR 4 1996

CENTRAL ISLIP PUBLIC LIBRARY

3 1800 00141 5583